Train to Win

Written by Samantha Montgomerie

Collins

Sled dogs are big and strong. They have an **instinct** to pull.

This sport is perfect for them. They like training on the trails.

The Arctic is freezing. Storms are bitter.
The **sweeping plains** are steep.

4

Sled dogs have thick coats to keep out the chill. They train so they can **endure** the trails.

"All right!" hollers the musher.
The dogs run at speed on
the trail.

musher

Sled dogs are smart. The musher trains the dogs to hear orders.

The dogs hear the signal to run.
They sprint off down the steep trail.

The dogs set the speed. Swing dogs tug the sled out from trees.

swing dogs

The sled speeds by the markers. The dogs strain harder. They speed off to win.

markers

The sled swoops to the finish.
The crowd claps. The dogs yelp.

Sled dogs train hard. Now they must sleep and wait to run again.

Glossary

endure put up with

instinct born to do it with no thinking

sweeping plains curving flat land

Trail map

Letters and Sounds: Phase 4

Word count: 170

Focus on adjacent consonants with long vowel phonemes, e.g. /s//p//ee//d/.

Common exception words: to, the, have, are, pull, all, by, they

Curriculum links: Geography: Human and Physical Geography; Science: Animals, including humans

National Curriculum learning objectives: Reading/word reading: apply phonic knowledge and skills as the route to decode words; read accurately by blending sounds in unfamiliar words containing GPCs that have been taught; Reading/comprehension: understand both the books they can already read accurately and fluently and those they listen to by making inferences on the basis of what is being said and done

Developing fluency

- Take turns to read a page, ensuring your child pays attention to full stops, and pauses before starting each new sentence.
- Encourage your child to read with an enthusiastic expression to emphasise the thrill of the sport.

Phonic practice

- Practise reading words ending in -ing by blending one chunk of the word at a time:

  train/ing   freez/ing   sweep/ing

- Challenge your child to read the following words ending in -er, in the same way:

  bitt/er   mush/er   ord/ers
  holl/ers   mark/ers   hard/er

Extending vocabulary

- Ask your child to suggest a glossary definition for the following words. Encourage them to check each word in its context first:

  sled (e.g. *a form of transport that slides across the snow*)

  trail (e.g. *a marked route through the snow*)

  musher (e.g. *person who race sleds pulled by dogs*)